W9-AJP-892

TEXAS

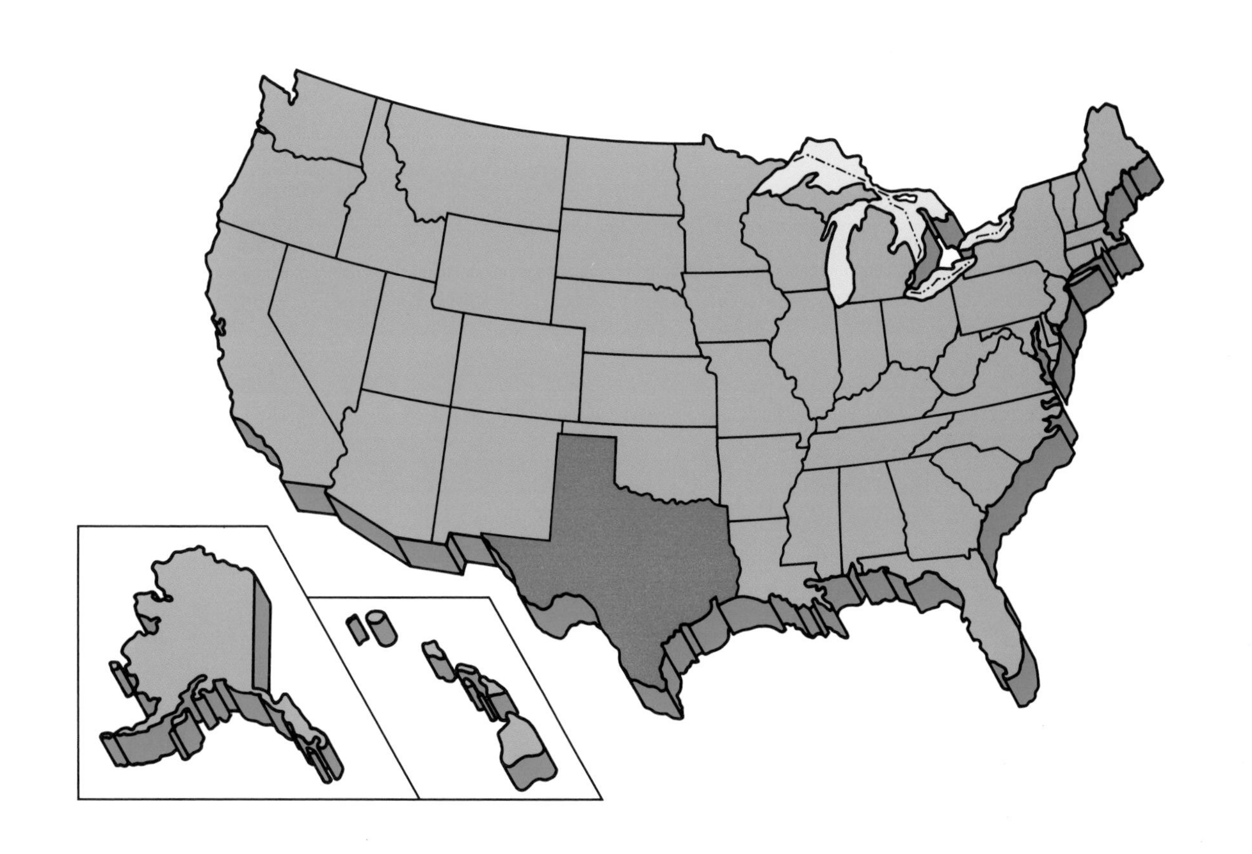

TEXAS

Kathy Pelta

Lerner Publications Company

This book is available in two editions:
Library binding by Lerner Publications Company
Soft cover by First Avenue Editions
241 First Avenue North
Minneapolis, MN 55401
ISBN: 0-8225-2749-9 (lib. bdg.)
ISBN: 0-8225-9667-9 (pbk.)

LIBRARY OF CONGRESS
CATALOGING-IN-PUBLICATION DATA
Pelta, Kathy.
Texas / by Kathy Pelta.
p. cm. — (Hello U.S.A.)
Includes index.
ISBN 0-8225-2749-9 (lib. bdg.)
1. Texas—Juvenile literature. [1. Texas.]
I. Title. II. Series.
F386.3.P45 1994
976.4—dc20
93-33390
CIP
AC

Manufactured in the United States of America
1 2 3 4 5 6 - I/JR - 99 98 97 96 95 94

Cover photograph by Buddy Mays / Travel Stock.

The glossary that begins on page 68 gives definitions of words shown in **bold type** in the text.

This book is printed on acid-free, recyclable paper.

Contents

PAGE CHAPTER

Did You Know . . . ?

❑ Hot, hotter, hottest! Texas produces more than half of all the jalapeño chili sauce made in the United States.

❑ Thousands of bats make their homes under the bridges in Austin, Texas. At first, people were afraid of the night flyers. But a program to tell folks about the good things bats do—such as eating tons of unwanted bugs every evening—has made Austin a bat lover's paradise.

❑ Texas holds the largest cattle ranch in the continental United States. The King Ranch in southern Texas covers more than 800,000 acres (323,760 hectares).

❑ Three of the world's most successful golfers—Ben Hogan, Babe Didrikson Zaharias, and Lee Trevino—were born in Texas.

❑ No one is quite sure why Stanley Marsh III, a rich rancher from northern Texas, put 10 Cadillacs nose down in a field near his ranch.

❑ Texas's most hunted bank robbers were Bonnie and Clyde. During a two-year period, this Texas-born pair committed a dozen murders and robbed many banks. In 1934 law officials ambushed the duo in Louisiana.

Near the city of Amarillo, 10 Cadillacs are half buried in the ground.

A Trip Around the State

The thundering hooves of stampeding cattle. The noisy clunk of oil-drilling equipment. A flowering cactus in a deserted landscape. These are sights and sounds that many people link to Texas. But this big, broad state—the second largest in the United States—also has mountains, grasslands, rivers, and miles of coastline.

Texas is a southern state, located midway between the Atlantic and Pacific oceans. Water shapes many of the state's borders.

A flowering cactus *(left)*, **a roseate spoonbill in flight** *(inset left)*, **and an old windmill** *(inset right)* **are common sights in Texas.**

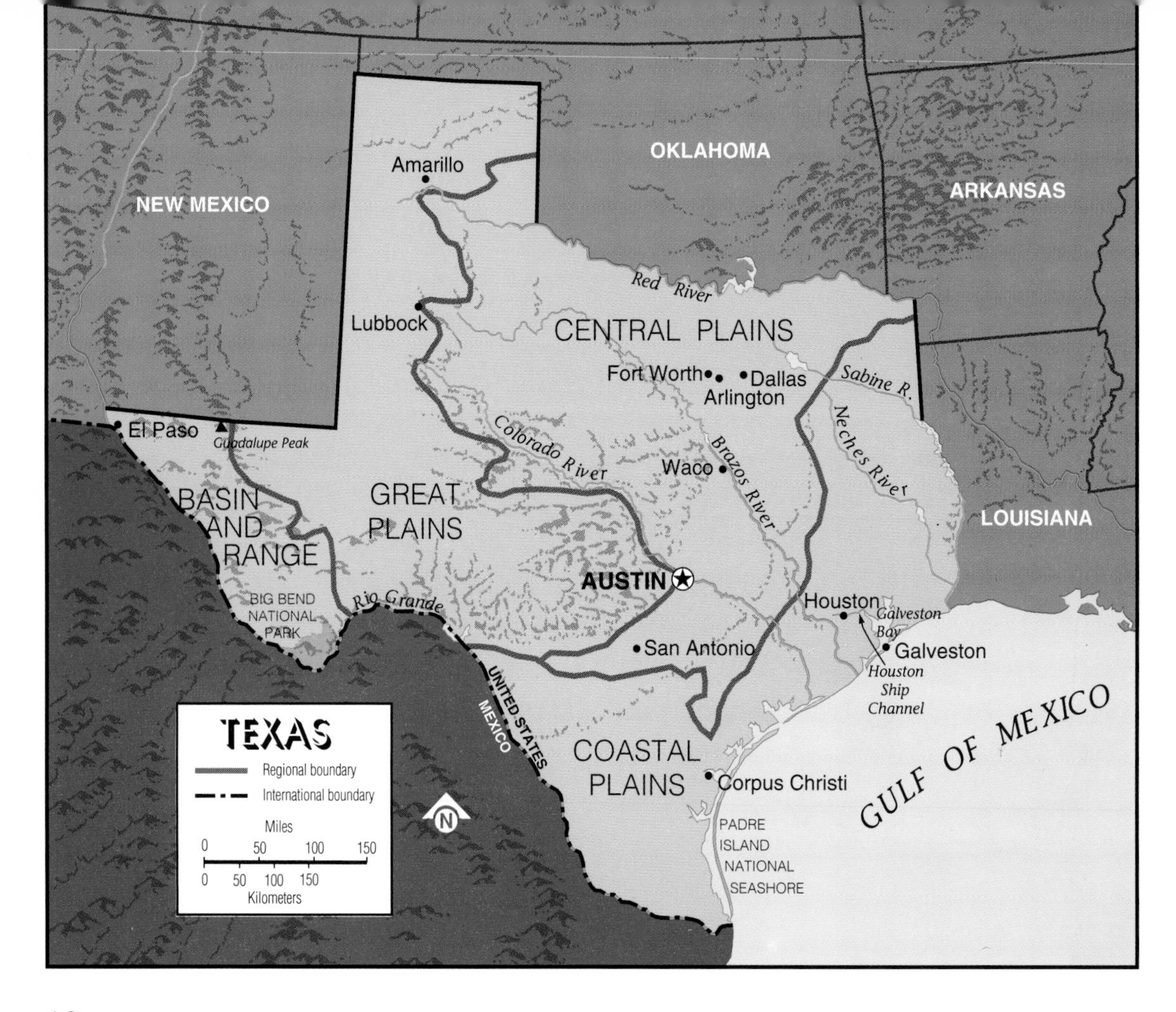
NEW MEXICO
OKLAHOMA
ARKANSAS
LOUISIANA
Amarillo
Lubbock
Red River
CENTRAL PLAINS
Fort Worth
Dallas
Arlington
Sabine R.
Neches River
Colorado River
Brazos River
Waco
El Paso
Guadalupe Peak
BASIN AND RANGE
GREAT PLAINS
AUSTIN
BIG BEND NATIONAL PARK
Rio Grande
Houston
Galveston Bay
Galveston
San Antonio
Houston Ship Channel
UNITED STATES
MEXICO
COASTAL PLAINS
Corpus Christi
GULF OF MEXICO
PADRE ISLAND NATIONAL SEASHORE
TEXAS
Regional boundary
International boundary
Miles
0 50 100 150
0 50 100 150
Kilometers
N

Across the Red River, Texas's northern neighbors are Oklahoma and Arkansas. To the east, across the Sabine River, is Louisiana. New Mexico lies to the west. To the southwest, beyond the Rio Grande, is the country of Mexico.

The Gulf of Mexico—part of the Atlantic Ocean—marks the southeastern boundary of Texas. Narrow **sandbars** (islands of sand) lie offshore and protect Texas's Gulf coast from storms and strong winds. Bays, including Galveston Bay and Corpus Christi Bay, sit between the sandbars and the coast.

Most of Texas's rivers empty into the Gulf of Mexico. The state's longest waterways are the Rio Grande and the Red, Brazos, and Colorado rivers.

Using a paddle for balance, a kayaker makes his way through the churning waters of the muddy Rio Grande.

Dams built across some rivers—such as the Neches and the Sabine—have created **reservoirs,** or artificial lakes. These lakes store freshwater for towns and cities throughout the state.

Four main land regions stretch across Texas. The land rises in height from the Gulf of Mexico to Texas's western border. The regions are the Coastal Plains, the Central Plains, the Great Plains, and the Basin and Range region.

The low Coastal Plains spread north and west from the Gulf and cover one-third of the state. Warm weather helps farmers in the southern Coastal Plains grow many kinds of fruits and vegetables year-round. To the north, along the eastern

Cabbages thrive in the warm climate of the southern Coastal Plains.

A bucking bronco decorates the pump of this oil well in Texas's Central Plains.

border with Louisiana, fields of cotton, sugarcane, and rice thrive in the rich soil.

West of the Coastal Plains lie the slightly higher Central Plains. Oil wells, farms, forests, and large cattle ranches share this rolling and rugged land with coyotes, foxes, and jackrabbits. In the 1800s, thousands of buffalo roamed here. Long before that, many dinosaurs did, too!

Even higher than the Central Plains are the Great Plains, which extend across most of western Texas. These plains are part of a vast region that stretches north all the way to Canada. Farmers on the Great Plains of Texas plant fields of wheat and cotton. Huge herds of cattle, goats, and sheep feed on the region's hearty grasses.

The Great Plains include the nearly treeless Texas Panhandle. The area is named for its shape. The Panhandle juts northward from the rest of Texas and, on a map, looks a little like the handle on a saucepan.

The only mountains in Texas rise in the Basin and Range region of the southwest. Within this area, Guadalupe Peak, the highest point in the state, reaches 8,751 feet (2,667 meters). In between the mountains are valleys that get little rainfall.

Huge sandstone rocks ***(above)*** **look down on the dry plains of the Texas Panhandle. The Chisos Mountains** ***(left)*** **add to the scenery in Big Bend National Park, part of the Basin and Range region.**

Within the Basin and Range region, porcupines, mule deer, and bears wander through the mountain wilderness, as do surefooted bighorn sheep. In dry areas, rattlesnakes and horned lizards look for shade beneath ocotillo shrubs and prickly pear cactuses.

It's probably no surprise that in a state as large as Texas, the

A bighorn sheep *(facing page, bottom left)* **suns itself in Big Bend National Park, where agave** *(facing page, top)* **and ocotillo** *(facing page, bottom right)* **plants abound.**

climate varies a lot from place to place. Warm, humid weather is typical on the Gulf coast. Hot, dry weather conditions are common in the southwest, while harsh winters chill the Texas Panhandle.

The Basin and Range region, the state's hottest area, averages 60° F (16° C) in January and 85° F (29° C) in July. In the Panhandle, where temperatures are cooler, January's average temperature is 35° F (2° C), and July's is 79° F (26° C).

Texas is hit by more tornadoes than any other state. Each spring and summer, around 100 of these destructive, funnel-shaped clouds touch down, mainly in northern Texas. Hurricanes often blow in from the Gulf and strike the southern coast and the nearby sandbars.

Although Texas doesn't get much **precipitation,** most of it comes in the form of rain. The state's average rainfall every year is 27 inches (69 centimeters). Most of the rain falls in the Coastal Plains. Hills in this region block rain clouds from moving farther inland. For this reason, much of the rest of Texas is dry. In some years, parts of southwestern Texas get only 7 inches (18 cm) of rain.

Texas's Story

The first people to live in what is now Texas probably came from the north more than 10,000 years ago. They were part of a large movement of people who crossed a land bridge from Asia to North America and then headed southward.

In Texas these early hunters and gatherers moved from place to place in search of wild plants and animals. They made strong containers and sharp weapons. With these tools, the people hunted and butchered mammoths (hairy elephants) and giant bison for food. On the walls of their caves, early residents of what is now Texas painted scenes of people and of important religious events.

Later groups gathered seeds from wild plants and began to grow cotton, corn, beans, and squash. As food supplies became more dependable, the people no longer had to travel long distances to find food.

Early inhabitants of western Texas drew pictures on the walls of their cave dwellings. These images are from the Panther Cave, which is named for a panther painting that is more than 15 feet (5 meters) long.

To find food, Karankawa Indians fished the Gulf of Mexico for oysters *(left)*. If the catch was small, the Karankawa sometimes ate lizards *(right)* to survive.

Native Americans, or Indians, are the descendants of these early hunters and farmers. By the year 1500, about 30,000 Indians from 20 different nations, or tribes, were living in what is now Texas.

Many of the Karankawa made their homes along the marshy Gulf coast. On foot or by canoe, these people searched the waters for oysters, clams, and turtles. When these animals were scarce, the Karankawa ate lizards, spiders, and worms.

In the woods and hills to the north and east of the Gulf coast lived Native American groups that spoke the Caddo languages. These people were skilled potters and hunters. They also planted large fields of corn, beans, and pumpkins. Among the Caddoan-speaking groups were the Tejas, whose name means "friend." The state of Texas takes its name from these Indians.

Early groups of Caddoan-speaking Indians built mounds, which were used for burials and other holy rituals.

The Apache and the Kiowa hunted buffalo across the vast Great Plains. These two nations belonged to a larger grouping known as the Plains Indians. Like hunters of other Plains Indian nations, the Apache and the Kiowa followed their prey on foot. While on the hunt, the Indians lived in tepees, which were easy to set up and take down quickly.

Indians in what is now Texas had the land to themselves until the early 1500s. At that time, the king of Spain sent explorers to claim what is now Mexico. Travel-

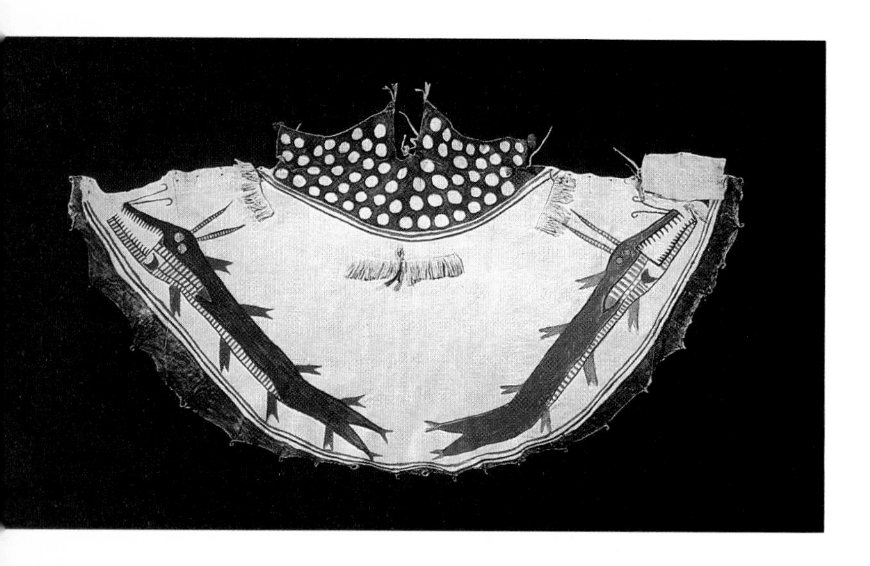

Kiowa tepees were often decorated with paintings. These pictures are from an ancient Kiowa story about a monster who waits underwater to trap swimmers.

Alonso Alvarez de Piñeda saw the twisting course of the Rio Grande *(right)*. Lost and hungry, Alvar Núñez Cabeza de Vaca *(inset)* asked a Karankawa for help in about 1528.

ing northward from Mexico, the Spaniard Alonso Alvarez de Piñeda reached the Rio Grande in 1519.

Nearly 10 years later, a shipwreck stranded another Spaniard, Alvar Núñez Cabeza de Vaca, along the Gulf coast. The Karankawa rescued him and told him legends about riches in cities north of the Rio Grande.

The tall bell tower of Mission San José, one of five Spanish missions in the city of San Antonio, is attached to a Roman Catholic chapel.

In the 1540s, Hernando de Soto searched what is now western Texas to find these legendary cities. But the Spaniard found no riches and reported his failure to the king of Spain. The king decided the region wasn't worth exploring anymore.

About 140 years later, however, Spanish priests urged the king of Spain to claim the lands north of the Rio Grande. The priests wanted to set up **missions** to teach the Catholic religion to the area's Indians. In 1682 a mission was built near what is now El Paso, in western Texas. In addition to the Catholic religion, the Europeans also brought horses, and the Indians soon began to use the animals. On horseback the Plains Indians could kill more buffalo, which they depended on for food, clothing, and other supplies.

By about 1700, the Spaniards had built dozens of missions, including one among the Tejas. Although the Tejas and some other Indian nations

Indian residents of Spanish missions went to religious services in the morning. During the rest of the day, the Indians worked on the missions' farms.

got along with the Europeans, many groups did not. For protection from these Indians, the Spaniards built a presidio, or fort, near each mission and stationed troops at the forts.

Sometimes farmers from Spain settled near the forts. These settlements eventually grew into towns. San Antonio, founded in 1731 near Mission San Antonio de Valero, was the first permanent European town in the land that the Spaniards began to call "Tejas."

The Spanish priests ran the missions by strict rules. Indian groups herded livestock or farmed to supply the missions with food. In time the Indians grew unhappy with the grueling work and rigid schedules at the missions. They missed the freedom to practice their own religions, to hunt game, and to plant their own foods.

Some Indians ran away from the missions. Many more died from measles and smallpox, diseases that the Indians had caught from the Europeans. Since the Indians had never been exposed to these illnesses, thousands died.

At the same time, a Plains Indian nation called the Comanche had moved onto the plains of what are now northern and central Texas. The Comanche were excellent horse riders and buffalo hunters. They didn't want Europeans to take over their hunting grounds on the Texas plains. To drive away Spanish settlers, the Comanche raided missions, burned farms, and stole horses.

By the late 1700s, Comanche attacks had scared most settlers into leaving. Fearful Catholic priests

After a successful buffalo hunt, Comanche women hung the meat to dry on racks. The women also scraped and flattened the animals' skins so the hides could be made into clothes or tepees.

During a buffalo hunt, Comanche men displayed their legendary horse-riding skills.

deserted the missions. In San Antonio, Spanish soldiers turned one of the missions into a presidio called the Alamo. For many years, few white settlers arrived in Texas, and most Indian groups returned to their traditional way of life.

This situation changed in 1821, after Mexico won its independence from Spain. The new Mexican government claimed Texas as Mexican territory. To strengthen this claim and to attract more settlers, the government offered free land to people who would come to Texas to live and work.

In the 1820s, Stephen Austin *(seated)* helped hundreds of farm families from the United States settle in southeastern Texas.

Many people in the United States were interested in the Mexican offer. Within months Stephen Austin, a U.S. businessman and politician, had arranged for nearly 300 U.S. families to settle in southeastern Texas.

Most of this small group, later known as the Old Three Hundred, were cotton farmers from areas in the southern United States. In addition to bringing farm tools, some of these settlers also brought black slaves, who were forced to labor in the cotton fields without pay.

BOTH SIDES OF THE STORY

In the 1820s, Stephen Austin's offer to give land in Texas to American settlers attracted people who were ready to make a new start. Members of his own family responded including a widowed cousin named Mary Austin Holley. Stephen set aside a piece of land on Galveston Bay for his cousin.

When Mary reached Texas, she immediately became enthused about the settlement. She wrote long letters to her family and friends, describing the landscape and climate of Texas in glowing terms. In one letter, Mary wrote, "The natural riches of this beautiful province have begun to be unfolded to the eyes of admiring adventurers. A new island has been discovered to delight the senses and enrich the pockets."

But a young Kentucky blacksmith, who arrived in Texas at about the same time, had a much different view. Noah Smithwick traveled inland to a settlement near San Antonio. "It was July, and the heat was intense," Smithwick noted in his diary. "The only water was swarming with mosquitos and full of malaria. Texas looked to me like a heaven for men and dogs, but a hell for women and oxen."

Cotton was one of the main crops that new settlers planted and harvested in Texas.

At first the new white settlers, or **Anglo Americans**, accepted being part of Mexico. By 1835, however, Mexico was under the strict rule of General Antonio López de Santa Anna, who was trying to control the U.S. settlers. He limited their freedom to travel and outlawed slavery. He also would not provide schools with teachers who spoke English.

The growing number of Anglo Americans in Texas disagreed with Santa Anna. They prepared to fight for their independence by forming a small volunteer army. In 1835, 200 members of this army defended the Alamo against 4,000 of Santa Anna's troops. Within two hours, nearly every person inside the Alamo was dead.

The next year, under their leader, Sam Houston, the remaining Texas volunteers won a second battle fought along the banks of the San Jacinto River. The Texans took Santa Anna prisoner and forced him to agree to Texas's independence.

Davy Crockett *(in above painting with raised gun)* **and other members of Texas's volunteer army defended the Alamo in 1835.** *(Right)* **After his loss at the Battle of San Jacinto, the Mexican general Antonio López de Santa Anna** *(center left in white trousers)* **surrendered to Sam Houston** *(lying down),* **who had been hurt in the fighting.**

Texas began to fly the Lone Star Flag in 1839, a few years after declaring independence from Mexico. The flag is named for the single star on the left side.

The Mexican government didn't approve of Texas's independence. But Texans adopted their own **constitution,** or set of laws, and elected Houston president of their country. They designed a flag with only one star on it and proudly flew the Lone Star Flag over public buildings.

The new nation got off to a shaky start. Although Texas had farms, it had few factories and little trade with other countries. Because Texas had so few goods to sell, it was poor. Houston and other Texans realized Texas couldn't afford to be independent, so they asked the

U.S. government to make Texas part of the United States.

While the U.S. government talked about this plan, covered wagons rumbled into eastern and central Texas—where farmland was available. The wagons brought settlers, many of whom were **immigrants** from Germany, France, and Poland. Not everyone welcomed the newcomers. The Mexicans, who still viewed Texas as part of Mexico, attacked them. So did the Comanche and the Kiowa.

The Petri family came from Germany to raise dairy cows and poultry in central Texas.

After 10 years of talking, the U.S. government allowed Texas to join the United States on December 29, 1845, as the 28th state. Because Mexico still claimed Texas, this event sparked the Mexican War. After two years of fierce fighting in both Mexico and Texas, U.S. troops defeated the Mexicans. By signing a peace **treaty**, or agreement, in 1848, Mexico gave up its claim to Texas, which became known as the Lone Star State.

Cotton was the new state's chief crop. Most farmers planted and harvested their own cotton fields, but some wealthy landowners had **plantations** (large farms) worked by slaves. Texas was one of many Southern states that allowed slav-

The U.S. Army battled Mexican troops during the Mexican War, which started after the United States made Texas the 28th state.

ery, a practice that Northern states had outlawed.

The issue of slavery sharply divided the United States. Northerners were trying to end slavery across the nation. Southerners wanted to keep owning slaves. In 1861 Texans voted to leave the Union. Texas joined other Southern states in a new country called the Confederate States of America, or the Confederacy. In the Confederacy, slavery remained legal.

The split between the North and the South led to the Civil War. More than 60,000 Texans joined military units in the Confederate army. Texas also provided guns, clothing, and food for Confederate troops. Cities such as Galveston, Dallas, and Houston grew, as new factories were built to make goods for the war.

The Civil War ended in 1865, and so did slavery. Many former slaves became **sharecroppers.** They worked on large farms for low wages and received tools and a small share of the crops.

After the Civil War, farmers were attracted by the vast farmland in western Texas and began moving there. The Comanche and the Kiowa tried to drive the newcomers away by attacking wagon trains and by burning farms. To protect the settlers, the U.S. Army raided the camps of Indian tribes.

Quanah Parker
A Man in Two Worlds

In 1836, during a Comanche raid on a white settlement in eastern Texas, Indian soldiers took a young settler named Cynthia Parker from her home. She adapted to the Native American way of life and eventually married a Comanche leader. Her son Quanah became one of the Comanche nation's most honored commanders.

As a young man, Quanah played down his white heritage by outshining other Comanche in the traditional activities of hunting and raiding. After attacks by the U.S. Army killed his father and captured his mother, Quanah organized more raids. His skill as a commander earned him the respect of Comanche far and wide.

But by 1875, the U.S. Army had forced most of Texas's Indians onto reservations run by white agents. Quanah, one of the last to surrender, was determined to get ahead in the white world but still keep his Indian roots. He became a strong voice for the Comanche, helping them earn money by renting their pastureland to white cattle ranchers. He also served as a judge in an Indian court and convinced white agents of the value of some Comanche traditions.

Within 10 years of arriving on the reservation, Quanah was regarded as his nation's leader. He often represented the Comanche in their dealings with the U.S. government. By the time of his death in 1911, Quanah was honored by many people in both the white and the Indian worlds.

Beginning in the 1870s, Texas cowboys drove herds of longhorn cattle northward to slaughtering houses in Kansas.

The soldiers forced thousands of Indians northward into Oklahoma, where the government had set aside a **reservation** known as Indian Territory. By 1875 the last of the Comanche and the Kiowa had moved to the reservation.

With few Indians remaining in the state, hundreds of ranchers came to the Great Plains of western Texas to raise longhorn cattle. Once the cows were fully grown, cowboys drove the herds through Texas and Oklahoma to Kansas.

The well drilled at Spindletop Hill in 1901 shot oil 200 feet (61 m) into the air.

In Kansas the animals were butchered or were shipped east by train. In the 1880s, after railroads were built in Texas, ranchers sent their cattle to Kansas by rail. The railways also carried Texas cotton to textile mills in the North to be made into cloth.

Ranchers and farmers grew rich from the sale of cattle and cotton. Some of the state's wealthiest people used their money to search for oil, which they had noticed in water wells throughout Texas. On January 10, 1901, drillers at Spindletop Hill near the Gulf coast struck a vast underground well of oil that gushed for nine days. Before long thousands of workers were pumping oil from many parts of Texas.

The world's demand for oil increased during World War I (1914–1918). Ships, planes, and other wartime vehicles needed this fuel, and Texas made millions of dollars by selling its oil.

The oil boom started other industries. Some companies made oil-drilling equipment. Others

A Lasting Mark

The tradition of branding—marking cattle with a lasting symbol to show who owns the animals—goes back to the beginnings of ranching in Texas. In the mid-1800s, ranchers didn't use fences to pen in cattle. The animals often roamed among herds belonging to neighboring ranches and sometimes wandered long distances in search of food. Branding was the only way to know which cattle belonged to which rancher. The unique markings also made it hard for cattle thieves, called rustlers, to sell stolen animals, because they could be traced back to the true owner.

Ranchers registered, or legally recorded, their brands. Books listed the appearance of the brands so people could quickly figure out who owned each animal. Roundup, the day cowboys gathered and branded newly born calves, was a special event that combined hard work with lots of food and lively music.

built ships to carry the fuel to worldwide markets. The Houston Ship Channel, which opened in 1914, allowed Houston's oil companies to send their oil to Galveston on the Gulf of Mexico.

Oil prices fell sharply in the 1930s during the Great Depression, a worldwide economic slump. As the oil industry slowed down, so did other businesses. Many Texans lost their jobs. Some wandered around the state looking for work or even just for a decent meal. Others left Texas altogether.

When World War II broke out in 1939, oil was in demand again, and Texas's economy boomed. During the war, military camps throughout the state trained many U.S. troops, pilots, and sailors.

8000 B.C. Ancestors of Native Americans are living in Texas

A.D. 1519 Alvarez de Piñeda reaches the Rio Grande

1682 Spain sets up its first mission in Texas

1731 San Antonio is established

1821 Mexico wins its independence from Spain and claims Texas

1835 Mexican troops defeat Texas volunteers at the Alamo

About 750,000 Texans served in the armed forces. Some of these Texans became military heroes. Audie Murphy from Kingston, Texas, won the most medals of any World War II soldier. Chester A. Nimitz of Fredericksburg, Texas, commanded all U.S. naval and marine forces in the Pacific Ocean from 1941 to 1945. In 1943 Dwight D. Eisenhower of Denison, Texas, was named head of all U.S. and Allied troops in Europe.

In 1953 Eisenhower became the first Texas-born president of the United States. Another Texan, Lyndon B. Johnson, served as vice president to John F. Kennedy.

1845 Texas becomes the 28th state
1901 Drillers strike oil at Spindletop Hill
1914 Houston Ship Channel is completed
1953 Dwight D. Eisenhower becomes first U.S. president from Texas
1963 John F. Kennedy is assassinated in Dallas
1990 Oil spill in Galveston Bay

Johnson became president after Kennedy was murdered in Dallas in 1963. Twenty-five years later, voters elected George Bush as president. He had lived and worked in Texas for many years.

In the late 1980s, the state that had grown rich on oil barely survived a sharp drop in oil prices. Other oil problems arose in 1990, when a serious oil spill polluted Galveston Bay. New industries—such as computer-chip factories and electronics firms—helped Texas's economy keep going. Although Texas still pumps oil, Texans now have other ways to make a living in the Lone Star State.

Living and Working in Texas

When Texas first became a state, most people made their homes on lone farms and ranches. Nowadays some Texans still live in rural areas, but four out of five residents are city dwellers.

Located in southeastern Texas, Houston is the state's largest city. Other big communities include El Paso in the far west, Corpus Christi in the south, and the cluster of

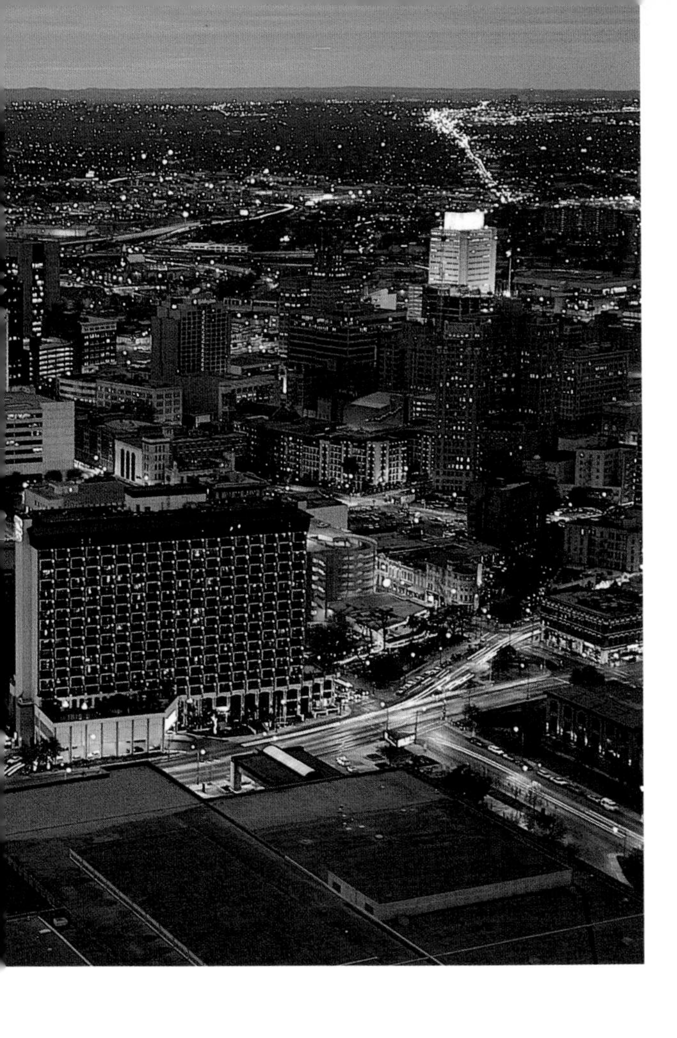

At dusk, lights twinkle throughout downtown San Antonio, where nearly one million Texans live.

Dallas, Fort Worth, and Arlington in north central Texas. Sizable cities in central Texas are San Antonio, Austin (the state capital), and Waco. In the Panhandle, Lubbock and Amarillo are the leading towns.

Texas is home to nearly 17 million people, and the number is rising. Only California and New York have more residents. About 61 percent of all Texans have European roots. These people are mainly descended from the German, French, and Polish farmers who settled in the territory in the 1800s.

Young Texans tumble in the courtyard of a plastic castle.

Another 25 percent of the state's growing population are **Latinos**, whose ancestors came mostly from Mexico. Some Latinos in the state have recently arrived from Mexico, while others can trace their roots to the time when Texas was part of Mexico. The majority of Texas's Latinos speak both Spanish and English.

Nearly 12 percent of all Texans are African American. Native Americans, who once were the only people living in Texas, make up less than 1 percent of the population. In recent years, immigrants from Vietnam, China, the Philippines, and South Korea have come to the state. They account for about 1 percent of Texas's population.

Texans celebrate their many cultures with food, festivals, and music. The German community of New Braunfels, for example, hosts traditional bands and dance groups at its autumn Wurstfest (Sausage Festival). During Fiesta San Antonio, crowds enjoy the city's Latino heritage with spicy Tex-Mex food, bands of strolling guitarists, and flower parades. Blues and gospel music help Texans salute Juneteenth, which honors the day that Texas's slaves were declared free. Texans also enjoy fiddling contests, rodeos, and chili cookoffs.

Ethnic events give Texans a chance to celebrate the state's many cultures. Here a woman sways to the music of a traditional Latino dance.

Dressed in a German costume, a guide *(far left)* **welcomes visitors to a park in San Antonio. The city's most famous event is Fiesta San Antonio, when floats** *(center)* **parade through the streets. Every autumn Corpus Christi hosts an outdoor fair that attracts young artists** *(above).*

Whether Texans want to study their state's colorful past or explore modern art, they can find just the right museum. The Witte Memorial Museum in San Antonio features exhibits on Indian communities and early Anglo American settlements. At Space Center Houston, visitors can see giant rockets, moon rocks, and movies that were filmed in space.

Texas is a sports fan's paradise. The state has a professional team to match almost every taste. The Texas Rangers and the Houston Astros dazzle baseball-loving crowds. The leaps and rebounds of the San Antonio Spurs and the Houston Rockets delight basketball buffs. Hockey fans cheer for the Dallas Stars. For football, Texans can root for the Houston Oilers or the Dallas Cowboys. College football also is a big crowd pleaser in Texas.

At Space Center Houston, visitors can see how astronauts move around in a spaceship.

Texans who enjoy the outdoors can fish, camp, or hike in 100 state parks and 5 state forests. Big Bend National Park is located in southwestern Texas, where the Rio Grande makes a sharp turn. The park's rugged mountains, steep canyons, and desert scenery show the untouched wilderness of the Basin and Range region.

Skateboarding on Padre Island *(top)* and canoeing down the Rio Grande *(left)* are popular outdoor activities in Texas.

Country-music groups perform on "Austin City Limits," a television show produced in the capital of Texas.

When Texans are not relaxing, they are on the job. About 76 percent of all working Texans have positions that provide services to people, businesses, and government. Some service workers are bank tellers, store clerks, hospital technicians, or schoolteachers. Others staff airports, hotels, museums, and restaurants. Some workers load and unload cargo at docks on the southern coast. Government employees include city and state officials, law enforcers, and park rangers.

Manufacturing employs about 14 percent of Texas's workforce. Many laborers package food items, including fruits, vegetables, beef, and dairy products.

A shrimper *(above)* in Corpus Christi checks his catch. The sun sets behind an oil rig *(right)* in western Texas.

Factories along the Gulf coast process shrimp, crab, and oysters brought in by fishing crews. Mill workers make paper and plywood from trees cut in the pine, oak, and hickory forests of northeastern Texas.

Workers in Dallas and Fort Worth produce aircraft, clothing, and oil-drilling equipment. Austin is a center for computer-chip manufacturing. Texas leads the nation in making chemicals, plastics, and other products from oil.

Texas's construction industry is thriving. A rise in the number of Texans has created a need for more houses, schools, roads, and businesses. About 5 percent of working Texans have jobs as carpenters, bricklayers, electricians, painters, and plumbers.

About 3 percent of the workforce in Texas is employed on farms or ranches. Texans raise most of the nation's beef cattle, sheep, and goats. The state is second only to California in the amount of sorghum (a cornlike grass), rice, and wheat it grows.

In the Texas Panhandle, farmers raise sorghum *(left)* and cattle *(inset)*.

Farmers in Texas also supply the nation with spinach, onions, potatoes, and melons. Peaches, oranges, and grapefruits ripen in the Rio Grande Valley. And Texas's cotton growers provide one-third of the nation's cotton.

The mining industry employs 2 percent of working Texans. Some miners in Texas search for oil and natural gas in underground fields throughout the state. Texas supplies one-fourth of the nation's oil and one-third of its natural gas.

Most people in the state's oil industry live in and around Houston, near the largest oil wells. Refineries near Houston purify the crude oil so it can be used as fuel.

Texas leads the United States in producing sulfur and limestone. Using heavy-duty machines, workers dredge (suck up) sand and gravel from the beds of Texas's rivers and bays. The sand and gravel can be used to make concrete and other building materials. Miners also dig

Far above the ground, a worker tightens machinery on an oil rig.

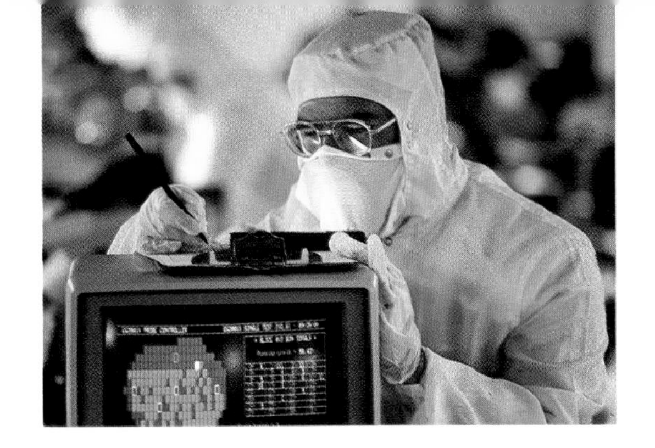

Fancy roping *(above)* is a traditional part of ranching in Texas. Modern parts of Texas's economy include high-tech companies that manufacture computers *(right).*

underground for coal, salt, gypsum, and talc.

Some working Texans have stayed with traditional industries, including ranching and oil. Other workers have helped the state expand into new areas of manufacturing, such as aircraft and computers. From rodeos to rockets and from chili to computer chips, Texas is changing with the times, as well as keeping its ties to the past.

Protecting the Environment

Located in southeastern Texas, Galveston Bay is one of the state's most important bodies of water. Every year the bay produces one-fourth of Texas's blue crab catch, one-third of its shrimp haul, and two-thirds of its oyster harvest. The Houston Ship Channel connects Galveston to Houston, where manufactured goods are loaded onto ships that exit through the bay to reach the Gulf of Mexico. In addition, oil refineries and chemical plants line the shores of the bay.

Offshore oil platforms *(left)* dwarf passing boats in Galveston Bay. Blue crabs *(below)* feed on algae (tiny life-forms) in the bay's protected waters.

One out of six Texans lives in the Galveston Bay area, which is also an important recreation center. Each year thousands of people come to watch graceful roseate spoonbills, snowy egrets, and great blue herons nest and feed on the marsh grasses at the bay's edge. Fresh seafood makes the bay's restaurants among the state's finest. Beaches lure sunbathers, while old ships attract history buffs.

Long-legged roseate spoonbills hatch and feed their young in marsh grasses along Galveston Bay.

The *Elissa* first sailed into Galveston Bay in 1883. After years of cargo service, the ship was left to rot. Restorers rescued the *Elissa,* which now cruises along the Gulf coast, attracting visitors to the bay area.

Fresh seafood draws people to restaurants throughout the bay area.

After an oil spill in July 1990 ***(left),*** **Galveston residents worked hard to clean up the bay's waters. A sign** ***(facing page)*** **warns people that underwater pipelines can leak chemicals into the bay.**

The buildup of people and industries has harmed Galveston Bay in many ways. Oil tankers have accidentally spilled large amounts of oil into the bay. The oil pollutes the water and sticks to the bay's wildlife, making it hard for the animals to swim, fly, or feed. Cities and factories have dumped poisonous chemicals into the water. These chemicals have killed birds and fish that live in or near the bay.

Machines dredge the bay's sand, gravel, and soil, which are then piled up to extend the shore. A wider shore gives builders more room to create housing with a view of the bay. But marsh grasses are uprooted when workers dredge the bay. When marsh grasses are pulled up, the marshes' birds lose a major food source and nesting ground. These animals either leave the area or starve.

Texans living near the bay have also polluted the water. Some residents pour household chemicals—such as used car oil and paint—down their drains. Through underground pipes, these pollutants eventually end up in the bay.

Another way people near Galveston Bay pollute the water is by putting too much fertilizer on their gardens and lawns. These chemicals help grass and other plants grow and stay healthy. Rain and water from lawn sprinklers wash off the extra fertilizer, sending it into storm drains. These underground pipes route the water into the bay. Water treatment centers try to filter out the pollutants before they reach the bay, but some chemicals cannot be removed.

A view from the air shows floating barriers called booms that were set up to try to keep the 1990 oil spill from spreading.

In the 1980s, concerned Texans saw signs of trouble in Galveston Bay—polluted water, lower seafood catches, and the loss of marsh grasses. These people met with city and state leaders, as well as with fishing and oil companies, to look for ways to save the bay. All sides agreed that a healthy bay made sense for the state's economy. Fishing would thrive, and birds would attract tourists. Homeowners would have an even more beautiful Gulf view to add to the value of their property.

Chemical plants around Galveston Bay are now more careful about how they get rid of their wastes. Governmental groups make sure that cities and factories dump only the legal amount of waste material into the bay. Companies rush to clean up oil spills with the latest equipment. Next to storm drains, residents have put up signs that read, "Dump no waste, drains to bay."

Fences protect newly planted marsh grasses from the action of waves and from animals.

Children, teenagers, and adult volunteers from the Galveston Bay Foundation are replanting lost marsh grasses. The foundation also educates families about how to protect the bay. Beach cleanups are popular yearly events. Texans hope that these actions will help preserve Galveston Bay for future generations to enjoy.

As part of Galveston Bay's annual beach cleanup, a mother and daughter bag litter.

Texas's Famous People

◀ ROSS PEROT

▼ CHARLES TANDY

HOWARD ◀ HUGHES

BUSINESS LEADERS

Howard Hughes (1905–1976), a native of Houston, made millions of dollars selling oil-drilling equipment in the 1920s. He used some of his wealth to produce and direct movies, such as *Scarface* and *The Outlaw.*

H. Ross Perot (born 1930) became a billionaire after selling Electronic Data Systems, the company that he had founded in 1962. A native of Texarkana, Texas, Perot highlighted his business skills in his unsuccessful campaign for U.S. president in 1992.

Charles Tandy (1918–1978), from Brownsville, Texas, bought the failing Radio Shack electronics stores in 1967. He made Radio Shack into a billion-dollar success by manufacturing and selling affordable computers for use at home.

▲ JOAN CRAWFORD

▼ STEVE MARTIN

ENTERTAINMENT FIGURES

Joan Crawford (1908–1973) was a Hollywood superstar whose acting career began with silent films. Originally from San Antonio, Crawford won an Academy Award in 1945 for her role in *Mildred Pierce.*

Steve Martin (born 1945) is an actor, writer, and producer from Waco, Texas. He gained fame in the 1970s for his work on the television show "Saturday Night Live" and later starred in many films, including *Roxanne* and *Father of the Bride.*

Gene Roddenberry (1921–1991) created "Star Trek," a popular television series of the 1960s. Born in El Paso, Roddenberry was a police officer before becoming a writer. His other television work includes scripts for "Dragnet" and "The Naked City."

▲ GENE RODDENBERRY

▼ JANIS JOPLIN

MUSICIANS

Buddy Holly (1936–1959), a native of Lubbock, Texas, was a singer, composer, and guitarist whose blend of country and rock and roll influenced many other musicians. Holly's best-selling songs include "Peggy Sue" and "That'll Be the Day."

Janis Joplin (1943–1970) was a rock and blues singer from Port Arthur, Texas. Her hits include "Ball and Chain" and "Piece of My Heart." The 1979 film *The Rose* is based on her life.

Roy Orbison (1936–1988) was a pioneer rock-and-roll singer, songwriter, and guitarist. His biggest hit, "Oh Pretty Woman," sold more than seven million copies. Orbison, a native of Vernon, Texas, was elected to the Rock and Roll Hall of Fame in 1987.

◀ BUDDY HOLLY

◀ ROY ORBISON

HENRY CISNEROS ▶

POLITICAL LEADERS

Henry Cisneros (born 1947), from San Antonio, served as mayor of his hometown from 1981 to 1988. Cisneros, the first Latino mayor of a major U.S. city, became U.S. secretary of Housing and Urban Development in 1993.

LYNDON JOHNSON ▶

▼ ANN RICHARDS

BARBARA JORDAN ▶

Lyndon B. Johnson (1908–1973), born in Stonewall, Texas, served as U.S. president from 1963 to 1969. While in office, Johnson pushed through the Civil Rights Act of 1964, which barred discrimination based on race, religion, or gender. His widening of the Vietnam War was unpopular and eventually led Johnson to retire from politics.

Barbara Jordan (born 1936) was the first African American woman from the South to be elected to the U.S. House of Representatives. Known for her fiery speaking skills, the Houston native was chosen to address the Democratic National Convention in 1976 and 1992.

Ann W. Richards (born 1933), from Lakeview, Texas, was elected the state's governor in 1991, becoming the second woman to hold that post in Texas. Richards's frank, funny speaking style is popular with voters.

▲ SHAQUILLE O'NEAL

▲ FRANK ROBINSON

SPORTS FIGURES

Shaquille ("Shaq") O'Neal (born 1972), center for the Orlando Magic basketball team, went to high school in San Antonio. O'Neal, who stands more than 7 feet (2 m) tall and weighs about 300 pounds (136 kilograms), was named the National Basketball Association's Rookie of the Year in 1993.

Frank Robinson (born 1935), manager of the Baltimore Orioles, is from Beaumont, Texas. The highlight of his long baseball career came in 1966, when he led the American League in batting average, home runs, and runs batted in. In 1975 Robinson became the first African American to manage a major-league team. He was elected to the Baseball Hall of Fame in 1982.

Nolan Ryan (born 1947) retired in 1993 as one of baseball's greatest pitchers. Raised in Alvin, Texas, Ryan signed with the New York Mets in 1965 and played later for the Houston Astros and the Texas Rangers. In addition to striking out more batters (5,714) than any other pitcher, Ryan threw a record seven no-hitters during his 27-year career.

Willie Shoemaker (born 1931) has won more horse races than any other jockey. In 1986 he became the oldest jockey to win the Kentucky Derby, one of horse racing's biggest events. Shoemaker, who retired in 1990, was born in Fabens, Texas.

▲ NOLAN RYAN

▼ WILLIE SHOEMAKER

▲ LARRY MCMURTRY

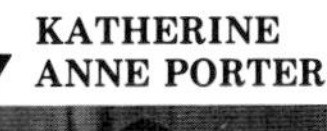

▼ KATHERINE ANNE PORTER

WRITERS

John Griffin (1920–1980), a white writer, underwent medical treatments to darken his skin and then lived in the South. His best-known book, *Black Like Me,* describes his experience of racial discrimination. After the book's publication in 1961, the Dallas native worked to ease communication between whites and African Americans.

Larry McMurtry (born 1936) comes from a long line of cattle ranchers in Wichita Falls, Texas. He used his family history to write the Pulitzer Prize–winning book *Lonesome Dove,* which later became a popular television miniseries. His other works include *Terms of Endearment* and *The Last Picture Show,* both of which were made into award-winning films.

Katherine Anne Porter (1890–1980), from Indian Creek, Texas, wrote short stories and novels, including *Ship of Fools,* which was made into a popular film in 1965. Her *Collected Stories* won a Pulitzer Prize in 1966.

Facts-at-a-Glance

Nickname: Lone Star State
Song: "Texas, Our Texas"
Motto: Friendship
Flower: bluebonnet
Tree: pecan
Bird: mockingbird

Population: 16,986,510*
Rank in population, nationwide: 3rd
Area: 268,601 sq mi (695,677 sq km)
Rank in area, nationwide: 2nd
Date and ranking of statehood: December 29, 1845, the 28th state
Capital: Austin
Major cities (and populations*): Houston (1,630,553), Dallas (1,006,877), San Antonio (935,933), El Paso (515,342), Austin (465,622), Fort Worth (447,619)
U.S. senators: 2
U.S. representatives: 30
Electoral votes: 32

*1990 census

Places to visit: Space Center Houston in Houston, the Alamo in San Antonio, Texas Ranger Hall of Fame in Waco, Panhandle Plains Historical Museum in Canyon, Padre Island National Seashore

Annual events: Cotton Bowl in Dallas (Jan.), Rattlesnake Round-up in Sweetwater (March), Old Fiddler's Reunion in Athens (May), All Girl Rodeo in Hereford (Aug.), State Fair in Dallas (Oct.), World Championship Chili Cookoff in Terlingua (Nov.)

Average January temperature: 49° F (9° C) **Average July temperature:** 84° F (29° C)

Natural resources: oil, natural gas, coal, sulfur, salt, limestone, uranium, forests, cement, sand and gravel

Agricultural products: beef cattle, cotton, sorghum, wheat, rice, hogs, pecans, sheep, onions, potatoes, soybeans, sugarcane, peaches, grapes, watermelons

Manufactured goods: computers and computer chips, electrical equipment, chemicals, plastics, machinery, packaged foods, communication systems, airplanes and other transportation equipment

ENDANGERED SPECIES

Mammals—gray wolf, black bear, black-footed ferret, ocelot, jaguar, blue whale, manatee

Birds—whooping crane, interior least tern, Attwater's greater prairie-chicken, ivory-billed woodpecker

Reptiles and amphibians—Big Bend mud turtle, Concho water snake, Texas blind salamander

Fish—Comanche Springs pupfish, Big Bend gambusia, Pecos gambusia

Plants—Texas snowbells, ashy dogweed, Texas trailing phlox, Texas poppy-mallow, Texas wild rice

[Texas]

WHERE TEXANS WORK

Services—59 percent
(services includes jobs in trade; community, social, & personal services; finance, insurance, & real estate; transportation, communication, & utilities)

Government—17 percent

Manufacturing—14 percent

Construction—5 percent

Agriculture—3 percent

Mining—2 percent

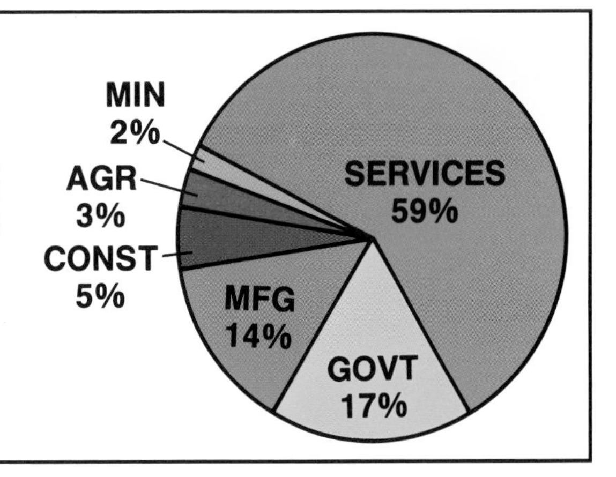

PRONUNCIATION GUIDE

Apache (uh-PACH-ee)

Cabeza de Vaca, Alvar Núñez (kah-BAY-thah day BAH-kah, AHL-bahr NOON-yayth)

Caddo (KAD-oh)

Comanche (kuh-MAN-chee)

de Soto, Hernando (dih SOH-toh, ehr-NAHN-doh)

Guadalupe (GWAHD-uhl-oop)

Karankawa (kuh-RANG-kuh-wah)

Kiowa (KY-uh-wah)

Piñeda, Alonso Alvarez de (pee-NYAY-dah, ah-LOHN-soh AHL-bah-rayth day)

Rio Grande (ree-oh GRAND)

Tejas (TAY-hahs)

Anglo American Historically, an English-speaking white person from the United States who lived in lands under Mexican rule.

constitution The system of basic laws or rules of a government, society, or organization. The document in which these laws or rules are written.

immigrant A person who moves into a foreign country and settles there.

Latino A person living in the United States who either came from or has ancestors from Latin America. Latin America includes Mexico and most of Central and South America.

mission The place where missionaries work. Missionaries are people sent out by a religious group to spread its beliefs to other peoples.

plantation A large estate, usually in a warm climate, on which crops are grown by workers who live on the estate. In the past, plantation owners usually used slave labor.

precipitation Rain, snow, and other forms of moisture that fall to earth.

reservation Public land set aside by the government to be used by Native Americans.

reservoir A place where water is collected and stored for later use.

sandbar An island of sand formed along a shore or in a river.

sharecropper A person who farms land that belongs to someone else. As payment for their labor, sharecroppers get a house, tools, and a share of the crops they grow.

treaty An agreement between two or more groups, usually having to do with peace or trade.

Index

Acknowledgments:

Maryland Cartographics, pp. 2, 10; Buddy Mays / Travel Stock, pp. 2–3, 7, 12, 15, 16 (top), 16 (bottom left), 46 (left), 48 (top and bottom), 52, 57 (right); Jack Lindstrom, p. 7; Lynn M. Stone, pp. 8 (inset), 20 (left and right), 55, 56; Root Resources: Ben Goldstein, pp. 8–9, James Blank, p. 24, Garry D. McMichael, p. 50 (right); Frederica Georgia, pp. 9 (inset), 11, 23, 49, 53 (left), 57 (left); © Robert & Linda Mitchell, pp. 13, 30; C. W. Biedel / Laatsch-Hupp Photo, pp. 14–15; Jerry Hennen, pp. 16 (bottom right), 42–43, 45, 51 (inset); Texas Memorial Museum, p. 19; Texas Highways Magazine, p. 21; Smithsonian Institution, p. 22; IPS, pp. 23 (inset), 27; Library of Congress, pp. 25, 34, 37; National Museum of American Art, Washington, D.C. / Art Resource, NY, p. 26; Daughters of the Republic of Texas Library at the Alamo, p. 28; Friends of the Governor's Mansion, Austin, p. 31 (top); Archives Div., Texas State Library, pp. 31 (bottom), 36; Russell Fish III / Texas Memorial Museum, p. 33; Dallas Historical Society, p. 38; Diane Cooper, p. 44; NE Stock Photo: Roger Bickel, pp. 46 (center), 50–51, Robert C. Dinu, pp. 54–55; Corpus Christi Area CVB, pp. 46 (right), 50 (left); © 1992 Space Center Houston, All Rights Reserved, p. 47; Texas Instruments, p. 53 (right); Gavin R. Villareal / Texas General Land Office, pp. 58, 60; Galveston Bay Foundation, pp. 59, 61 (left); © Andrew Hammar, p. 61 (right); Perot '92, p. 62 (top left); Tandy Corp., p. 62 (top center); Hollywood Book & Poster, pp. 62 (top right, bottom left, and bottom right), 63 (top left, top center, top right, and bottom left); Mayor's Office, City of San Antonio, p. 63 (bottom right); MN DFL Party, p. 64 (top); Texas Governor's Office, p. 64 (top center); Charles Guerrero / Guerrero Photographic Group, p. 64 (top right); Pepsico, Inc., p. 64 (bottom left); Baltimore Orioles, p. 64 (bottom right); Texas Rangers, p. 65 (top left); Churchill Downs, Inc. / Kinetic Corp., p. 65 (top right); Diana Lynn Ossana, p. 65 (bottom left); Univ. Archives, Univ. of NC-Greensboro, p. 65 (bottom right); Jean Matheny, p. 66; Houston Astros, p. 69; Patty Leslie / Center for Plant Conservation, p. 70.